fMM

KIDS GET CODING

OUR DIGITAL WORLD

Heather Lyons & Elizabeth Tweedale

WAYLAND

Contents

Getting started   3

What can a computer do?   4

Inputs and outputs   6

All kinds of content   8

Storing and naming   10

Bits and bytes   12

Searching and sorting   14

Pixel perfect   16

In the movies …   18

Sound it out   20

Extension activities   22

Words to remember   23

Activity answers   23

Index   24

Getting started

Hi! I'm Data Duck! We are going to learn about the digital world around us. Let's go!

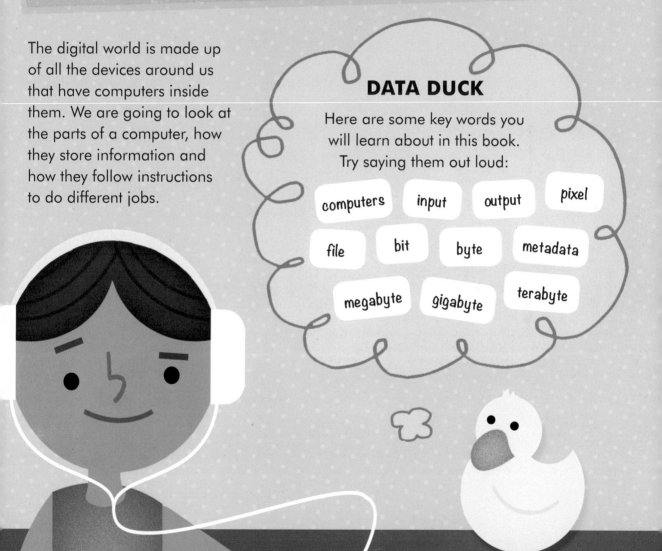

The digital world is made up of all the devices around us that have computers inside them. We are going to look at the parts of a computer, how they store information and how they follow instructions to do different jobs.

DATA DUCK

Here are some key words you will learn about in this book. Try saying them out loud:

computers input output pixel

file bit byte metadata

megabyte gigabyte terabyte

There are lots of activities in the book for you to try out. There are also some online activities for you to practise. For the online activities, go to **www.blueshiftcoding.com/kidsgetcoding** and look for the activity with the page number from the book.

{3}

What can a computer do?

A computer is a type of machine. It can't think like us but it can store information and follow instructions. We can use computers to book cinema tickets, watch videos and find information to help us with our schoolwork.

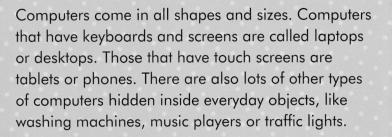

Computers come in all shapes and sizes. Computers that have keyboards and screens are called laptops or desktops. Those that have touch screens are tablets or phones. There are also lots of other types of computers hidden inside everyday objects, like washing machines, music players or traffic lights.

Helpful machines

What are some of the things you do with a computer? Can you make a list like the one below?

- We can use computers to look up things on the Internet.

- We can use computers to write stories or draw pictures.

- We can use computers to help us with our maths homework and make graphs and charts.

DATA DUCK

When you start looking at the world around you, you quickly discover it is full of computers! Can you work out which devices near you have computers inside them, and which don't?

Inputs and outputs

There are many different parts to a computer. Some parts store information and other parts let us see and hear information.

Camera
This puts information about what the computer 'sees' into the computer, so it is an input device.

Processor and memory
Computers store files and programs in their memory. When we give a computer instructions, the processor (which is a bit like a brain) follows them and shows us information on the screen. It is not an input or an output device.

Screen
This is an output device. Programs use the computer screen to display information.

Keyboard
The keyboard is used to put information into the computer: it is an input device.

Mouse
We use the mouse to select things on the screen or to move them around. It is also an input device.

Speaker
Information (sound) comes out of the speaker, so it is an output device.

DATA DUCK

An input device is what we use to send information into the computer. An output device is what we use to see or hear information sent out from the computer.

In or out?

The kids on this page are all doing different activities. Can you decide who is putting information into the computer (input) and who is receiving information from the computer (output)?

Turn to page 23 to see the answers.

PAGE 2 OF 3...

All kinds of content

Computers can store school presentations, music, movies, stories, pictures and games. Just about anything! These things are all different types of digital content.

Computers store and save things in a file. We then need special programs (sometimes called 'applications') to open these files and look at the content.

There are special programs for every sort of content: programs for reading and writing words, for looking at pictures, for watching videos or listening to music, and even for browsing the Internet.

Different types of files have different letters at the end of their names. These letters tell us what kind of file they are and what kind of program can open them. Some of the letters you may have seen include:

.pdf (a document with pictures and words)

.html (a web page)

.doc (a Word document)

.jpeg (a picture)

These letters at the end of a filename are called extensions.

DATA DUCK

These letters at the end of a filename are called extensions.

Matching

In the green boxes are types of content. In the red boxes are sorts of programs. Can you match the right program with the right content?

Turn to page 23 to see the answers.

Story

Presentation

Poem

Photo

Movie

Web page

Song

Web browser

Music player

Video player

Picture editing program

Slideshow program

Writing program

Storing and naming

When we save our work on a computer, it is saved as a file. We need to give our file a name that we can remember so that we can find it when we want to open it again.

When naming a file on a computer that other people have access to, we should call it something we will remember, and that won't be confused with anyone else's. For example: DataDuck_DucklingStory.doc.

There are different places on our computer where we can save our work. The Desktop is what we see when we turn on our computer. We can save our work here, but if there are lots of files it gets messy – a bit like your bedroom if you don't put your toys away!

DATA DUCK
I like to include my name and information about what's inside my file.

There are other places that we can save our files. When we're at school, we might have a special folder with our name on it. We may also have special folders for saving certain types of stuff, like photos or music.

Remember, when saving files, think about what important information should be included so they can be found again.

The name game

Let's practise naming files. What would you call the following sorts of things? Where would be a good place to save them?

A story about your summer holidays.

A presentation about space.

A picture of a tree.

A web page about football.

Turn to page 23 to see the answers.

Bits and bytes

The computer's brain (remember, it's called a 'processor'), will follow a program's instructions and work things out by turning little switches on and off.

The files and programs we store on computers are made up of 0s and 1s. The computer understands 0 and 1 because it knows 0 is off and 1 is on.

For example, if we were to tell a computer to write the letter A, the processor would store the letter as 01000001, because this is how the computer understands A.

Each 0 and 1 is called a 'bit'. Can you count how many bits there are in the letter A that the computer is storing?

A

01000001

DATA DUCK
When we store files, we need to think about the amount of space they take up in the computer's memory because we don't want to run out of room!

The smallest unit of memory is a bit. 8 bits make **1 byte**.

1,000 bytes make **1 kilobyte (KB),** which is enough storage for a page of writing.

Which is the biggest?

Can you sort the following file sizes in order from smallest to biggest?

- 20 kilobytes (20 KB)
- 2 gigabytes (2 GB)
- 10 bytes
- 10 megabytes (10 MB)
- 500 kilobytes (500 KB)

Turn to page 23 to see the answers.

1,000 kilobytes make **1 megabyte (MB),** which is enough storage for a photo.

1,000 megabytes make **1 gigabyte (GB),** which is enough storage for a TV show.

1,000 gigabytes make **1 terabyte (TB),** which can store up to 4 million photos!

USB 3.0

COMPUTER MEMORY

Searching and sorting

When we save a file, we store lots of information about that file at the same time. This means there is lots of information we can search for when we need to find the file again.

When we look for a book on a shelf, we look for the book title – but we might also look for the colour of the book or the picture on the front. It is the same when we look for computer files: there is lots of information we can use to help us search. This information is called 'metadata'.

Some of the information that will always be shown with the name of our file includes the date we made it, its size, where it is saved and its extension.

DATA DUCK

Remember, the 'extension' is the end part of a file name which shows the type of file that it is. We can sort and search by this information as well.

Sorting metadata

Can you work out the answers to the questions below using this file list?

What is the newest file?

What is the biggest file?

What is the smallest file?

Turn to page 23 to see the answers.

Name	Date modified	Size	Kind
AstronautStory.doc	Today 13:54	100 KB	Microsoft Word document
Penguins.jpg	11 August 16:19	3.3 MB	JPEG image
Timetable.xls	2 March 14:16	11 KB	Microsoft Excel workbook
Chapter2.pdf	7 November 11:08	230 KB	Adobe PDF document
My Stuff	Yesterday 09:37	- -	Folder
FlyingAKite.mov	6 February 17:49	47 MB	QT movie

Pixel perfect

Let's look at some of the ways a computer stores the pictures we view on it, and how programs read the information to show us pictures.

When we look at pictures on a computer screen, we are actually looking at millions of little dots called 'pixels'. These pixels can be turned on or off, and every single one can show us millions of colours.

Each one of these pixels has a specific location on the screen. For example, in this image, the pixel in the very top left of the grid might be called 0,0 whilst another one towards the middle of the screen might be called 6,8.

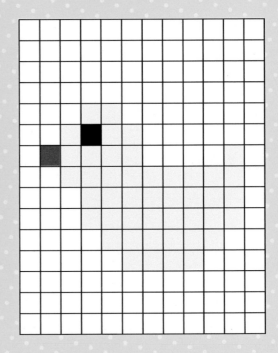

When we save a picture file, we save the colour and location for every pixel. When a picture program opens a photo file it reads the information stored there.

On and off

Imagine you have a computer screen that can only show black and white pictures. Its pixels can either be on (white) or off (black).

Data Duck has been a bit sneaky and turned on some pixels that he shouldn't have!

On a piece of paper, write down the number of each of the pixels you need to turn off to complete the smiley face.

Turn to page 23 to see the answers.

DATA DUCK
Remember, when we turn a pixel off, it goes black.

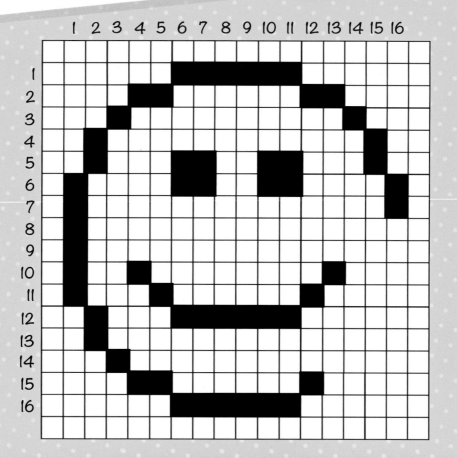

In the movies ...

Now that we understand how computers show us pictures, we can start to find out what we can do with pictures.

A video is a set of thousands of pictures that are shown very, very quickly one after the other.

When we look at a video, we are looking at 30 different pictures shown every single second. When we look at pictures that are shown very quickly one after the other, it looks like the images in the pictures are moving.

What is happening at 00:03:20?
What is happening at 00:03:40?

00:03:10

00:03:20

00:03:30

00:03:40

DATA DUCK
Don't forget that videos also have sound! When the computer plays a video, it knows exactly which sound should be played with each picture.

Make a flipbook

Let's have a look at how pictures can change using a flipbook.

Divide an A4 piece of paper into eight by folding it in half, then half again, and then in half again. Unfold it so it lies flat, then cut the paper along the fold lines so that you have eight pieces.

Draw a picture of a rocket on the first piece of paper. Then, draw the rocket again on the second piece of paper, slightly more to the right. Keep drawing a rocket on each piece of paper, moving it to the right each time.

Now, put all of the pieces together in order from first to last. Fix them together on the left edge and flip quickly through the pages. You've made your first flipbook!

Can you make another flipbook to create a story?

Sound it out

Now that we understand how pictures and videos are made, we can look at another type of content: sound!

Have you ever seen a funny picture that looks like this?

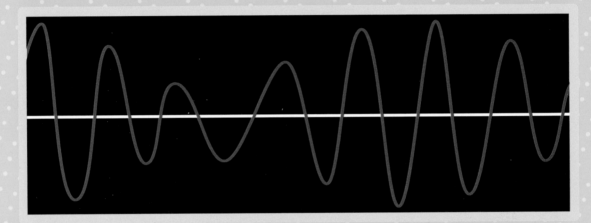

This is how a computer understands sound. The lines going up and down are called 'sound waves'. The waves that are taller will make a louder sound, while shorter waves will be quieter. Waves that are close together are high notes, while waves that are further apart are lower notes.

We can use the computer to change sounds too, such as noises we record with a microphone or songs that we save to our computer.

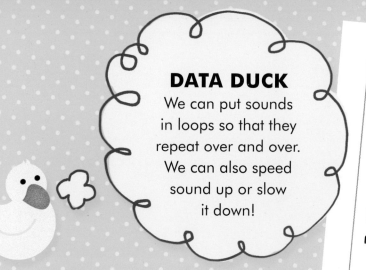

DATA DUCK

We can put sounds in loops so that they repeat over and over. We can also speed sound up or slow it down!

Decode the wave

Below is a sound picture showing different sorts of waves.

Which waves are the lowest notes? Which waves would make the loudest sound? Which waves would make the quietest sound?

Turn to page 23 to see the answers.

Go to **www.blueshiftcoding.com/kidsgetcoding** to try out a sound editing exercise!

Extension activities

Go to **blueshiftcoding.com/kidsgetcoding** for more fun activities and to practise:

- creating and editing pictures, games, videos and sound files
- making pixel pictures
- creating flip books to tell a story

Words to remember

extension	a part that is added to something.
input	something that puts information into a computer, such as a mouse.
output	something used to send information out of a computer such as a printer.
file	the name given for something used to store information on a computer.
bit	the smallest unit of memory on a computer (it is equal to "0" or "1").
byte	8 bits.
kilobyte	1,000 bytes.
loop	a series of steps with the final step connected to the first step, so the steps are repeated.
megabyte	1,000 kilobytes.
memory	a means of storing information in a computer.
metadata	information about other information. For example, information about a file on a computer (such as date created and type of file).
pixel	a small dot used on a computer screen to display text or images. It can be turned on or off and given one of a number of millions of colours.

Activity answers

Page 7

Playing a game -- we are using the controller to move our players: INPUT

Writing a story: INPUT

Watching a movie: OUTPUT

Taking a photo: INPUT

Listening to music: OUTPUT

Printing a story: OUTPUT

Page 9

Presentation: slideshow program

Poem: writing program

Photo album: picture editing program

Movie: video player

Web page: web browser

Song: music player

Page 11

The name for each file should explain what it is. You should put it in a place that makes sense, either in a folder belonging to you, or in a folder for that type of file.

If you are sharing a folder with other people, you should include your name in the filename. For example, if Data Duck was sharing his folder with other ducks, he might write: DataDuckSummerStory.doc and save it in the 'Stories' folder on his school computer.

Your answers might be a bit different, but your filenames could have been:

SummerHoliday.doc, saved in Stories folder
Tree.jpeg, saved in Pictures folder
SpacePresentation, saved in Schoolwork folder
FootballWebPage, saved on the Desktop.

Page 13

10 bytes, 20 kilobytes, 500 kilobytes, 10 megabytes, 2 gigabytes.

Page 15

Newest file: AstronautStory.doc
Biggest file: FlyingAKite.mov
Smallest file: Timetable.xls

Page 17

(13,15), (14,14), (15,13), (15,12), (16,11), (16,10), (16,9), (16,8).

Page 21

The C waves are the lowest notes.

The A waves would make the loudest sound.

The B waves would make the quietest sound.

Index

camera 6

device 3, 5–7

extension 9, 14

file 3, 6, 8–16

keyboard 4, 6

memory 6, 12

mouse 6

processor 6, 12

program 6, 8, 9, 12, 16

screen 4, 6, 16, 17

speaker 6

First published in Great Britain in 2016 by Wayland

Editors: Annabel Stones and Liza Miller
Illustration: Alex Westgate
Freelance editor: Katie Woolley
Designer: Anthony Hannant (LittleRedAnt)

ISBN: 9780750297011
10 9 8 7 6 5 4 3 2 1

Wayland
An imprint of
Hachette Children's Group
Part of Hodder & Stoughton
Carmelite House
50 Victoria Embankment
London EC4Y 0DZ

An Hachette UK Company
www.hachette.co.uk
www.hachettechildrens.co.uk

Printed in China